Remarkable Writers

Beverly Cleary

Susan Ring

www.av2books.com

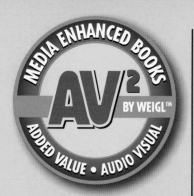

AV² provides enriched content that supplements and complements this boo[k]
Weigl's AV² books strive to create inspired learning and engage young min[d]
in a total learning experience.

Your AV² Media Enhanced books come alive with...

Audio
Listen to sections of the book read aloud.

Key Words
Study vocabulary, and complete a matching word activity.

Video
Watch informative video clips.

Quizzes
Test your knowledge.

Embedded Weblinks
Gain additional information for research.

Slide Show
View images and captions, and prepare a presentation.

Try This!
Complete activities and hands-on experiments.

... and much, much more[!]

Go to **www.av2books.com**, and enter this book's unique code.

BOOK CODE

X179261

AV² by Weigl brings you media enhanced books that support active learning.

Published by AV² by Weigl
350 5th Avenue, 59th Floor
New York, NY 10118

Website: www.weigl.com www.av2books.com
Copyright ©2015 AV² by Weigl
Library of Congress Control Number: 2013953167

ISBN 978-1-4896-0656-3 (hardcover)
ISBN 978-1-4896-0657-0 (softcover)
ISBN 978-1-4896-0658-7 (single user eBook)
ISBN 978-1-4896-0659-4 (multi-user eBook)

Printed in the United States of America, in North Mankato, Minnesota
1 2 3 4 5 6 7 8 9 0 18 17 16 15 14

012014
WEP301113

Senior Editor: Heather Kissock
Design: Terry Paulhus

Weigl acknowledges Getty Images, Corbis, and Alamy as its primary photo suppliers for this title.

Contents

Introducing Beverly Cleary

Author Beverly Cleary is just as interesting as the characters in her children's books. Is it possible for someone who refused to read books as a little girl to become a best-selling children's author? It is possible, because Beverly Cleary did just that. As a young girl, Beverly disliked reading. However, with some help and encouragement, she soon became an **avid** reader. When she was young, Beverly noticed that there were not many books about ordinary children like herself. Many years later, she began to write funny books that children could **identify** with. Her characters are fun, ordinary children, much like her devoted readers.

Beverly's mother was a librarian who helped instill Beverly's love for reading. Today, many librarians and teachers pass along their love of Beverly's books to other readers.

A Little Sister
Goes A Long Way.

Joey KING
Selena GOMEZ

Ramona and Beezus

GENERAL AUDIENCES

 Actress Joey King brought Ramona Quimby's quirky personality to life in the 2010 film adaptation of the Ramona series, *Ramona and Beezus*.

Beverly Cleary writes children's books about everyday situations. One of Beverly's most popular characters is Ramona Quimby. She is a funny, bothersome, and brave little girl. Readers of all ages laugh out loud at Ramona's silly antics. Read on to find out more about the life and work of Beverly Cleary, one of the most popular children's book authors of all time.

Writers are often inspired to record the stories of people who lead interesting lives. The story of another person's life is called a biography. A biography can tell the story of any person, from authors such as Beverly Cleary, to inventors, presidents, and sports stars.

When writing a biography, authors must first collect information about their subject. This information may come from a book about the person's life, a news article about one of his or her accomplishments, or a review of his or her work. Libraries and the internet will have much of this information. Most biographers will also interview their subjects. Personal accounts provide a great deal of information and a unique point of view. When some basic details about the person's life have been collected, it is time to begin writing a biography.

As you read about Beverly Cleary, you will be introduced to the important parts of a biography. Use these tips and the examples provided to learn how to write about an author or any other remarkable person.

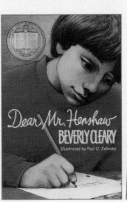

BEVERLY CLEARY
RAMONA'S WORLD

Ramona takes on fourth grade!

Dear Mr. Henshaw
BEVERLY CLEARY
Illustrated by Paul O. Zelinsky

BEVERLY CLEARY
RIBSY

Ribsy is lost
and having the adventure of his life!

Early Life

Beverly Cleary was born Beverly Atlee Bunn in McMinnville, Oregon. Chester and Mable Bunn, Beverly's parents, welcomed her into the world on April 12, 1916. Beverly's early childhood was spent living on the family farm in Yamhill, Oregon. Today, the Yamhill farm is a place that Beverly remembers with much fondness.

"When I write I do not think about writing for children. I write the stories that I enjoy telling and feel that I am most fortunate that children enjoy reading them."
— *Beverly Cleary*

As long as she followed her father's rules of safety, Beverly could do whatever she liked on the farm. A curious and active child, young Beverly was always up to something. She spent her days playing around the apple trees and the hen house on the farm. In Yamhill, Beverly learned much about nature. Her father taught her the names of local wildflowers. Her mother would sometimes take a break from her busy day to bring Beverly on nature walks. They would wander through fields and orchards. They would often come across wild animals, such as deer.

The fertile farmland and apple orchards of Yamhill County, Oregon, served as Beverly's home and early childhood playground.

Beverly's determination was as strong as her curiosity. She was also apt to take adults' words a little too seriously. One day, Beverly's father tried to give her a lesson in geography. Eager to teach her about planet Earth, he used an orange to demonstrate that the world is round. He traced an imaginary circle around the orange with his finger. He told Beverly that she could travel completely around the world and end up where she had started.

Several months later, when the Bunn family was enjoying a picnic in the outdoors, Beverly bolted across the field. Her father shouted after Beverly, asking her where she was going. She replied, "Around the world, like you said." Little Beverly was swiftly carried back home. Beverly Clearly has continued to show this determination and curiosity. In fact, these qualities can be found in many of the characters in Beverly's books.

✏ Beverly infused the character of Ramona Quimby with her own childhood curiosity, spontaneity, and quick-wit.

Writing About
Early Life

A person's early years have a strong influence on his or her future. Parents, teachers, and friends can have a large impact on how a person thinks, feels, and behaves. These effects are strong enough to last throughout childhood, and often a person's lifetime.

In order to write about a person's early life, biographers must find answers to the following questions.

1 Where and when was the person born?

2 What is known about the person's family and friends?

3 Did the person grow up in unusual circumstances?

Growing Up

One of Beverly's favorite pastimes was listening to her mother tell stories and read to her. Mable would read classic tales to her daughter, such as "The Three Little Pigs," and "Little Red Riding Hood." While Beverly enjoyed listening to stories, she did not enjoy reading them. She had a hard time learning to read. Also, finding books in Yamhill was difficult because the small town had no library. Beverly's parents could not afford to buy books, so Beverly's first picture books were magazine advertisements, such as Jell-O recipes.

> While Beverly enjoyed listening to stories, she did not enjoy reading them. She had a hard time learning to read.

More than anything, Beverly's mother wanted to have a library in Yamhill. She knew that having a library would provide the town's residents with great educational opportunities. By donating books, townspeople helped Mable realize her dream. Before long, the state of Oregon began donating books as well. Mable Bunn became the very first librarian of the town. Although she was busy, Mable continued to read to Beverly every evening. Today, Beverly is grateful for her mother's strong example and for passing on her love of reading.

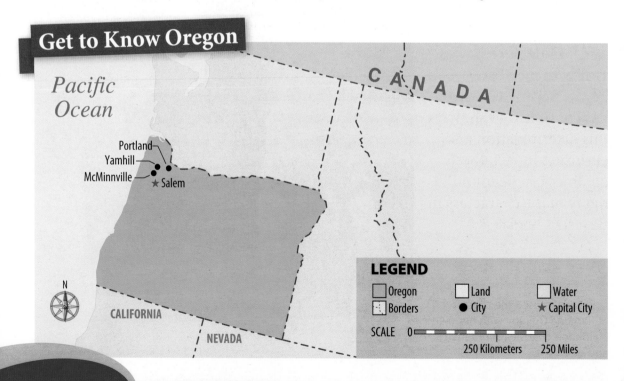

Get to Know Oregon

Pacific Ocean

CANADA

Portland
Yamhill
McMinnville
★ Salem

N

CALIFORNIA

NEVADA

LEGEND

☐ Oregon   ☐ Land   ☐ Water
⬚ Borders   ● City   ★ Capital City

SCALE 0 ⊢━━━━━━┤
                250 Kilometers   250 Miles

It was very difficult for Beverly's family to make a living by farming. When Beverly was 6 years old, the Bunns sold the farm in Yamhill. They moved to Portland, Oregon. Beverly's way of life changed overnight. While Portland was a big city, it did not take long for Beverly to feel at home there. She enjoyed living on Portland's Klickitat Street. There were many more children living in her new neighborhood than there had been in Yamhill.

Before long, Beverly started Grade 1. She had been excited about going to school, but Grade 1 was not easy for her. Beverly still found reading a challenge. This made her fear school, especially reading. However, Beverly was determined to learn. By Grade 3, with much practice, reading became easier for her. Before long, Beverly started reading everything that she could find.

📖 Portland is Oregon's largest city. It has a population of about 600,000 people.

Writing About Growing Up

Some people know what they want to achieve in life from a very young age. Others do not decide until much later. In any case, it is important for biographers to discuss when and how their subjects make these decisions. Using the information they collect, biographers try to answer the following questions about their subjects' paths in life.

1 Who had the most influence on the person?

2 Did he or she receive assistance from others?

3 Did the person have a positive attitude?

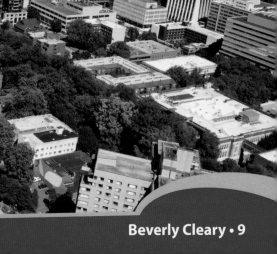

Developing Skills

By the time Beverly entered high school, she had become an avid reader. While books were a great escape, they could not shelter her from the effects of the **Great Depression** in the 1930s. Beverly's father lost his job as a guard at the local bank. The Bunns were barely able to provide for themselves.

Writing stories brought joy to Beverly during these difficult times. In high school, Beverly wrote a story called "The Diary of a Tree Sitter" for an English writing assignment. She took her mother's advice and made the story simple and funny. Beverly received an excellent grade. Her English teacher told her that she was a talented writer.

"I remember the group of grubby little boys, nonreaders, who came once a week during school hours. 'Where are the books about kids like us?' they wanted to know."
—*Beverly Cleary*

During the Great Depression, between 13 and 15 million Americans were unemployed. Many had to line up on the street to receive meals from charities.

After Beverly graduated high school, Beverly left home to study at the University of California in Berkeley. While there, she made many friends and attended parties and dances. At one party, Beverly met her future husband, Clarence Cleary. After Beverly graduated university, she studied to become a librarian.

In 1940, Beverly began working as a librarian in Yakima, Washington. She began to notice a troubling trend. Many children, especially young boys, did not like reading the children's books on the library's shelves. They found many of the stories outdated and unbelievable. Beverly began to wonder if she could write books that children found interesting.

📖 The University of California at Berkeley is made up of 14 different colleges and schools. Approximately 36,000 students attend classes there.

Timeline of Beverly Cleary

1950
Beverly's first novel, *Henry Huggins*, is published.

1940
Beverly becomes a children's librarian in Yakima, Washington.

1916
Beverly Cleary is born on April 12 in McMinnville, Oregon.

1938
Beverly graduates from the University of California.

1955

Beverly's twins, Malcolm and Marianne, are born.

2000

The Library of Congress names Beverly Cleary a 'Living Legend' for her contributions to children's **literature**.

1984

Beverly receives the Newbery Medal for *Dear Mr. Henshaw*.

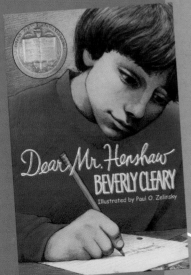

1999

Ramona's World is published.

Early Achievements

Beverly's writing skills began to develop at a young age. She gained early writing experience with school assignments. When Beverly was reading, she would always pay close attention to the things she liked and disliked in the story. These **observations** stayed in her memory and helped Beverly later in her writing career.

"I recalled my own childhood reading, when I longed for funny stories about the sort of children who lived in my neighborhood."
—*Beverly Cleary*

When Beverly was in Grade 7, her class was given an assignment to write a short story. Beverly wrote an imaginative story about feeding her pet chicken to George Washington's soldiers. Her teacher praised her writing and read the story aloud to the class. This gave Beverly the confidence to continue writing. Beverly attended Grant High School in Portland. She wrote articles for her high school newspaper and continued to excel at writing in her English classes. However, Beverly did not do much of her own creative writing. Most of the things she wrote were for school assignments. Beverly did not explore creative writing until much later in life.

Grant High School opened in 1924 with about 1,200 students. Today, more than 1,600 students attend the school, making it the largest high school in the city.

When she started working as a librarian, Beverly saw that there was a need for different kinds of children's books. Children did not seem to be interested in what was available. Beverly wondered why all the books written for children were based on unbelievable events and characters. Beverly remembered that she had wanted to read funny books about regular children when she was a child. She had wanted to read books with characters like the children living on Klickitat Street. In high school, the school librarian told Beverly that she should write books of her own someday.

Beverly's experience as a librarian inspired her to start writing children's books. Working around children allowed Beverly to see first-hand how they responded to different books.

Writing About
Early Achievements

No two people take the same path to success. Some people work very hard for a long time before achieving their goals. Others may take advantage of a fortunate turn of events. Biographers must make special note of the traits and qualities that allow their subjects to succeed.

1 What was the person's most important early success?

2 What processes does the person use in his or her work?

3 Which of the person's traits was most helpful in his or her work?

📖 Beverly's job as a librarian put her in contact with children on a daily basis. Talking to them about books and reading helped her when she began her writing career.

Tricks of the Trade

There are no strict rules for writing children's books. Every author has his or her own style and skills. The following are a few tips and **guidelines** that Beverly Cleary uses to help her write:

Make Writing a Habit

All skills get better with practice, including writing skills. Beverly Cleary suggests that to become a better writer, working every day is important. Begin by setting aside just 10 minutes a day to write, at the same time of day. This will help make a habit out of writing. By making writing a habit, writers will reach their goals with ease.

"If you don't see the book you want on the shelves, write it."
—*Beverly Cleary*

Beverly remains passionate about reading. Her home features artwork that demonstrates her feelings toward books.

Read, Read, Read

The more people read, the easier it becomes for them to learn about different styles of writing. Just as importantly, they get the opportunity to discover the kinds of books they like and dislike. Beverly believes that reading is great preparation for becoming a writer.

Tell a Story

A book is simply a story that has been written down. This is how Beverly views the writing process. Beverly imagines herself telling her story to an eager audience. She imagines the audience is sitting right in front of her. Then, Beverly writes down the words that she said to her make-believe audience.

Beverly tells children that many of her ideas come from her own childhood experiences.

Use Your Own Experiences

Fiction can be based on real people and events. Many of Beverly Cleary's ideas are drawn from her own childhood experiences. Adventures from Beverly's childhood remain clear in her mind, and she brings them to life in her writing. Her books are not completely **autobiographical**. Still, many of Beverly's childhood experiences can be found in her books. For instance, like Ramona, Beverly once tied cans to her feet and walked around the neighborhood. She also had many adventures with her friends on Klickitat Street.

Remarkable Books

Beverly Cleary has written books for all levels, from preschool to young adult. She has even written two autobiographies. Her autobiographies are called *A Girl From Yamhill* and *My Own Two Feet*. They are as delightful, funny, and interesting to read as her children's books. Above all, Beverly Cleary is known for her humorous books for children.

Henry Huggins

Henry Huggins is Beverly's first published book. It is about a young boy, Henry Huggins, who feels that his life is dull. He thinks that nothing exciting ever happens to him. This all changes when Henry comes across a stray dog on the street. Henry names the dog "Ribsy" because the dog is so skinny that his ribs stick out. Henry cannot leave poor Ribsy on the street, so he decides to take him home. However, getting home is more difficult than Henry had expected. Henry and Ribsy have many adventures along the way. Before the story concludes, readers are introduced to Henry's friends on Klickitat Street, including Beezus and her little sister, Ramona.

Beezus and Ramona

Henry Huggins has many neighborhood friends living around Klickitat Street. Beezus and her little sister, Ramona, are two of his friends. This book focuses on the relationship between these two sisters. Beezus finds her little sister **unbearable**. Ramona is always making trouble and getting all of the attention. Beezus struggles to deal with her mixed-up feelings for her irritating, yet adorable, little sister. When Ramona invites her entire kindergarten class over to her house without telling her mother, the trouble really begins.

Ribsy

Ribsy, Henry Huggins's dog, is the star of this humorous story. In this book, Ribsy gets hopelessly lost in a shopping mall parking lot. It is raining heavily, the pavement is slippery, and drivers are swerving to avoid him. Finally, Ribsy finds the Hugginses' car, jumps inside, and falls asleep. However, he has not jumped into his family car after all. Ribsy is taken to a different home, and a new family adopts him. Ribsy is heartbroken. He misses his owners and wants to find his real home. He especially wants to get back home to Henry. Ribsy's new owners call him "Rags." He does not like his new name. Finally, Ribsy escapes. He has many adventures and causes many disruptions as he wanders around in search of Henry. He visits a classroom and joins a school football game. Will Ribsy ever find Henry? Readers will not be able to put this book down until they find out.

BEVERLY CLEARY
RIBSY

Ribsy is lost . . . and having the adventure of his life!

Ramona Quimby, Age 8

Ramona's humorous antics make for fun reading. At 8 years of age, Ramona feels like a grown up. She rides the bus on her own and looks after little Willa Jean after school. However, Ramona is having a more difficult time at school. The latest trend in the schoolyard is to crack a hard-boiled egg on your head. By mistake, Ramona's mother sends her to school with the wrong kind of egg. To Ramona's embarrassment, she winds up cracking a raw egg on her head. While waiting to get cleaned up at the school office, Ramona overhears her teacher call her a **nuisance**. Ramona is very hurt by this remark. She cannot erase it from her mind. How will Ramona handle this situation?

Life as a third grader is tough!

AWARDS
Ramona Quimby, Age 8
1982 Newbery Honor Book
1975 Laura Ingalls Wilder Award

Ramona takes on fourth grade!

Ramona's World

Ramona Quimby is entering Grade 4. She expects it to be the best school year of her life, especially because she has a new best friend, Daisy. However, the year turns out to be more complicated than she had expected. At school, she is teased by a **mischievous** boy that she calls Yard Ape. She is also having trouble in spelling. At home, she feels pressured by her parents. They expect her to be a good **role model** for the new baby in the family. Plus, Ramona's older sister, Beezus, is always receiving praise. Somehow, Ramona manages to turns her year around.

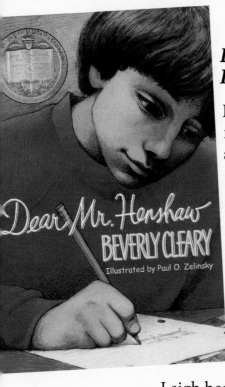

Dear Mr. Henshaw

Leigh Botts is the new kid in town and is trying desperately to fit in. To make matters worse, his parents are recently divorced, and he has just lost his dog. Leigh is struggling to understand why his parents divorced. He is also living in a new neighborhood and trying to make a new life for himself. Leigh is upset at his father, who does not visit or telephone. Feeling very lonely, Leigh decides to write a letter to Mr. Henshaw, his favorite author. As he gets older, Leigh begins to write to "Dear Mr. Pretend Henshaw" in his diary. It gives him comfort and a place to express his feelings. This book deals with some sad issues, but it is a page-turner.

The Mouse and the Motorcycle

Malcolm, Beverly Cleary's son, loved motorcycles when he was in Grade 4. His interest served as the inspiration for the character, Ralph S. Mouse. Beverly wrote three adventure stories based on Ralph S. Mouse. The mouse lives in a hotel room, eating the crumbs left behind by the many families that have stayed in Room 215. When a family stays overnight at the Mountain View Inn, the young son, Keith, leaves a toy motorcycle in the hotel room. He does not know that Ralph, a talking mouse, lives in the room. Ralph discovers the motorcycle and goes for a spin. He ends up falling into the wastebasket by accident. Keith finds Ralph S. Mouse. Keith shows Ralph how to ride the motorcycle safely. While riding the motorcycle is fun, it is also dangerous. Will Ralph be able to stay out of harm's way?

From Big Ideas to Books

Beverly's most popular books were published when she was an adult. However, the first time that she was published, Beverly was just a young girl. She even received a prize of $2 for her story. A local store sponsored a children's writing contest. The contestants were instructed to write a story about an animal of their choice. Beverly chose to write about the beaver. As it turned out, she was the only person who entered the contest. This did not dampen Beverly's excitement over winning. She also learned a great lesson. Beverly learned that in order to accomplish anything, you have to at least try. She realized that many people talk about writing, but only a few actually sit down and write.

> "Quite often somebody will say, 'What year do your books take place?' and the only answer I can give is, in childhood."
> —Beverly Cleary

Many years after the contest, Beverly took her own advice and sat down to write. She felt inspired to write when she and her husband found a pile of typing paper in the closet of their new home. She began working on a book for children like those she met working as a librarian in Yakima.

The Publishing Process

Publishing companies receive hundreds of **manuscripts** from authors each year. Only a few manuscripts become books. Publishers must be sure that a manuscript will sell many copies. As a result, publishers reject most of the manuscripts they receive. Once a manuscript has been accepted, it goes through

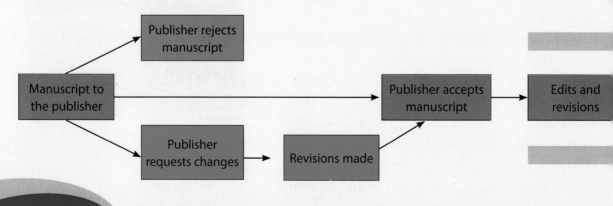

Beverly Cleary was in her thirties when she wrote her first book. Writing a children's book was a wise decision. The book, called *Henry Huggins*, was about a boy from Portland. Beverly based the character of Henry on the regular children who came to the library. Luckily, the first publisher she sent the manuscript to accepted it. The publishing company was called Morrow Junior Books. *Henry Huggins* was published in 1950 and was an instant success. Before long, librarians just like Beverly were loaning out *Henry Huggins* to eager young readers.

Beverly's parents did not approve of her marrying Clarence Cleary. Despite this, Beverly eloped with Clarence, and the two were married for 64 years. Clarence died in 2004.

many stages before it is published. Often, authors change their work to follow an editor's suggestions. Once the book is published, some authors receive royalties. This is money based on book sales.

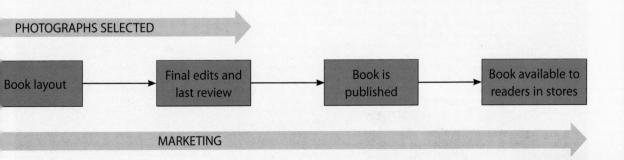

PHOTOGRAPHS SELECTED

Book layout → Final edits and last review → Book is published → Book available to readers in stores

MARKETING

Beverly Cleary Today

Over the years, Beverly has written more than thirty children's books. Beverly's most recent book, *Ramona's World*, was published in 1999. It is the latest addition to the popular Ramona series. These books are humorous tales about Ramona Quimby's many adventures. The release of *Ramona's World* thrilled dedicated fans. They were pleased to read about their favorite character again. Beverly's fans were treated to a film version of Ramona Quimby when *Ramona and Beezus* was released in 2010.

In 2011, Beverly Cleary announced that she would not be writing any more books. She hopes her fans have found enough enjoyment from the many books she has already published. Today, Beverly Cleary lives in Carmel, California, near the Pacific Ocean. Beverly now spends much of her spare time sewing and reading. She has two grown children, Malcolm and Marianne. Marianne plays the cello for a living, and Malcolm works as a banker.

Beverly currently resides in Carmel, California's "Jewel City," which has served as a haven for writers, poets, artists, musicians, and intellectuals for more than a century.

Since becoming a popular children's author, Beverly has traveled back to her home state of Oregon many times. When she visits Portland today, things look quite different. Grant Park, which is a few blocks away from where Beverly grew up, now has statues of Ramona Quimby, Henry Huggins, and his dog, Ribsy. More than 1,000 people, including Beverly, attended the **unveiling** of the Grant Park statues in 1995.

In 1996, Beverly attended the unveiling of two more statues. Both are representations of one of her most popular characters, Ramona Quimby. These statues are housed in the public library in Gresham, Oregon. Sculptor Lee Hunt captured Ramona's lively, humorous personality in these life-sized figures.

✍ "Friends of Henry and Ramona," a group comprised of Portland, Oregon teachers, librarians, and business people, formed in 1991 to raise money to build the *Beverly Cleary Sculpture Garden for Children*. The sculptures are located in Grant Park, where Beverly played as a child.

Writing About the Person Today

The biography of any living person is an ongoing story. People have new ideas, start new projects, and deal with challenges. For their work to be meaningful, biographers must include up-to-date information about their subjects. Through research, biographers try to answer the following questions.

1 Has the person received awards or recognition for accomplishments?

2 What is the person's life's work?

3 How have the person's accomplishments served others?

Fan Information

Beverly Cleary has won many awards for her outstanding writing and her lasting contribution to children's literature. In 1957, she won the Young Reader's Choice Award. She has also been given the Dorothy Canfield Fisher Children's Book Award. In 1984, Beverly was the United States author nominee for the International Hans Christian Andersen Award. In 2000, the Library of Congress named Beverly a "Living Legend" for her contribution to children's literature.

Beverly Cleary's books are available in more than twenty countries around the world. They can be read in fourteen different languages. Her books have been made into television programs in Japan, Sweden, and Spain.

Beverly Cleary received a National Medal of Arts by the United States government in 2003. President George W. Bush presented Beverly with the medal, the highest award given to artists in the United States.

Beverly Cleary has fans all around the world. Children continue to write to Beverly to tell her how much they love her books. Sometimes young fans suggest story ideas to Beverly. She has, at times, used her fans' suggestions in her books.

Ever since she wrote her first children's book, Beverly Cleary has gained many devoted fans. Some of her fans have gone on to become successful authors themselves. Authors such as Judy Blume consider Beverly's books to be a major influence on their own work and careers. Several websites have been created to honor Beverly and her books. The internet is a great place to find out more about the life of this fascinating author.

🖰 Readers and fans of Beverly's books can visit her website to learn more about the characters from her books, play games, and view an interactive map of Ramona Quimby's neighborhood.

Write a Biography

All of the parts of a biography work together to tell the story of a person's life. Find out how these elements combine by writing a biography. Begin by choosing a person whose story fascinates you. You will have to research the person's life by using library books and reliable websites. You can also e-mail the person or write him or her a letter. The person might agree to answer your questions directly.

Use a concept web, such as the one below, to guide you in writing the biography. Answer each of the questions listed using the information you have gathered. Each heading on the concept web will form an important part of the person's story.

Parts of a Biography

Early Life

Where and when was the person born?

What is known about the person's family and friends?

Did the person grow up in unusual circumstances?

Growing Up

Who had the most influence on the person?

Did he or she receive assistance from others?

Did the person have a positive attitude?

Developing Skills

What was the person's education?

What was the person's first job or work experience?

What obstacles did the person overcome?

Person Today

Has the person received awards or recognition for accomplishments?

What is the person's life's work?

How have the person's accomplishments served others?

Early Achievements

What was the person's most important early success?

What processes does the person use in his or her work?

Which of the person's traits were most helpful in his or her work?

Test Yourself

1 Where and when was Beverly Cleary born?

2 Where was the family's farm located?

3 Where did Beverly's family move when she was 6 years old?

4 What university did Beverly attend?

5 What kind of work did Beverly do before she became a writer?

6 What is the name of Beverly's first children's book?

7 What are the names of Beverly's twin children?

8 Where does Beverly currently live?

9 On what street do the characters in many of Beverly's children books live?

10 What is the name of Beverly's final published book?

ANSWERS
1. Beverly Cleary was born on April 12, 1916 in McMinnville, Oregon. 2. Yamhill, Oregon 3. The family moved to Portland, Oregon. 4. Beverly went to the University of California in Berkeley. 5. Beverly was a librarian. 6. *Henry Huggins* 7. Malcolm and Marianne 8. Carmel, California 9. Klickitat Street in Portland, Oregon 10. *Ramona's World*

Writing Terms

The field of writing has its own language. Understanding some of the more common writing terms will allow you to discuss your ideas about books.

action: the moving events of a work of fiction

antagonist: the person in the story who opposes the main character

autobiography: a history of a person's life written by that person

biography: a written account of another person's life

character: a person in a story, poem, or play

climax: the most exciting moment or turning point in a story

episode: a scene or short piece of action in a story

fiction: stories about characters and events that are not real

foreshadow: hinting at something that is going to happen later in the book

imagery: a written description of a thing or idea that brings an image to mind

narrator: the speaker of the story who relates the events

nonfiction: writing that deals with real people and events

novel: published writing of considerable length that portrays characters within a story

plot: the order of events in a work of fiction

protagonist: the leading character of a story; often a likable character

resolution: the end of the story, when the conflict is settled

scene: a single episode in a story

setting: the place and time in which a work of fiction occurs

theme: an idea that runs throughout a work of fiction

Key Words

autobiography: a written account of one's own life

avid: very eager or enthusiastic

Great Depression: a period of economic hardship that lasted from 1929 to the 1940s

guidelines: information about how something is done

identify: to connect with, or understand, another

literature: writing of lasting value, including plays, poems, and novels

manuscripts: drafts of stories before they are published

mischievous: playful but troublesome

nuisance: someone who is naughty or a pest

observations: details that are noticed

role model: a person who serves as inspiration to others

unbearable: difficult to deal with

unveiling: a ceremony in which something new is shown to the public for the first time

Index

Log on to www.av2books.com

AV² by Weigl brings you media enhanced books that support active learning. Go to www.av2books.com, and enter the special code found on page 2 of this book. You will gain access to enriched and enhanced content that supplements and complements this book. Content includes video, audio, weblinks, quizzes, a slide show, and activities.

AV² Online Navigation

Book Pages
AV² pages directly correspond to pages in the book.

Audio
Listen to sections the book read alo

Video
Watch informativ video clips.

Key Words
Study vocabulary, and complete a matching word activity.

Embedded Weblink
Gain additional information for research.

Try This!
Complete activities and hands-on experiments.

Quizzes
Test your knowledge.

Slide Show
View images and captions, and prepare a presentation.

AV² was built to bridge the gap between print and digital. We encourage you to tell us what you like and what you want to see in the future.

Sign up to be an AV² Ambassador at www.av2books.com/ambassador.